W9-AVH-542

SALT & PEPPER SHAKERS III

Identification and Values

Helene Guarnaccia

COLLECTOR BOOKS
A Division of Schroeder Publishing Co., Inc.

The current values in this book should be used only as a guide. They are not intended to set prices which may vary from one section of the country to another. Auction prices as well as dealer prices vary greatly and are affected by condition as well as demand. Neither the Author nor the Publisher assumes responsibility for any losses that might be incurred as a result of consulting this guide.

Photographs by Michael La Chioma
Proprietor: Hot Shots, Stratford, Connecticut

Additional copies of this book may be ordered from:

Collector Books
P.O. Box 3009
Paducah, KY 42002-3009

@$14.95. Add $2.00 for postage and handling.

Copyright: Helene Guarnaccia, 1991

This book or any part thereof may not be reproduced without the written consent of the Author and Publisher.

1 2 3 4 5 6 7 8 9 0

Table of Contents

Acknowledgments

I would like to thank all the people who have written to me and encouraged me to do this third book. It's hard to believe that there are still so many shakers out there that have not appeared in the five books already written on the subject. I have seen many extensive collections and still get just as excited when I find a set that I've never seen before.

I borrowed a few sets from the collection at Boothe Memorial Park in Stratford, Connecticut. They have a fabulous display set in a large glass case, with squirrels climbing trees, boats on a lake, etc. It is very artistically done, and well worth a visit. I also borrowed several pairs from the collection of Charlene Wallace of Bridgeport, Connecticut. I very much appreciate the trust and confidence shown me.

I would like to thank Norma Smith, of New York City, for her help. At a time when I was really bogged down about getting the book typed she came to my rescue. After working on her job five days a week, she opened her office on a Saturday and put 100 captions on the word processor. This was just the impetus I needed, and I went home, did the last 100 captions, and finished the book. Thank you, Norma!

I have had innumerable requests for Book I. The very first book that I did was a small book in black and white; a limited number was printed by the publisher, and its primary purpose was to test the market. The book was never reprinted, but I included everything in it in Book II.

I am still fascinated by the variety of people who collect, and the variety of their collections. I have seen wonderful tableaus made from salt and pepper shakers: zoos, sports arenas, circuses, etc. I have also been thrilled to hear from collectors as far away as New Zealand (my book was on display in the Auckland Library!); I correspond with collectors in Canada and Great Britain, and saw my book on the shelf in the Antique section of Foyles' bookstore in London. Even if the shakers themselves weren't so interesting, the people who collect them certainly are. Keep the letters coming...I love hearing from you all!

Advertising

A Campbell's ad with the Campbell Kids shakers. Advertising shakers appeal to both advertising and salt and pepper collectors. They are interesting because in many cases it is possible to research them.

TOP: Harvestore silos. They are marked A O Smith System. I bought these in Ohio and thought they were prevalent in the Midwest. On my next trip to Vermont I noticed that almost every silo was a royal blue Harvestore...salt and pepper shakers certainly increase one's awareness.

BOTTOM: These are two different sets of Borden's Elsie the cow. The paper label on the white set adds to its value.

TOP: Mitchell's Dairy milk bottle shakers. Mitchell's Dairy was run by Elnathan Mitchell and by his father before him. It was a local Connecticut dairy bought out by Bordens in the late 1940's or early 1950's. Bordens closed its operations in Connecticut in the mid 1970's.

CENTER: Wade's Dairy milk bottles with plastic shaker tops. Wade's Dairy was founded in 1893 and is still operating in Fairfield County in Connecticut. There are still 3 members of the Wade family in the business: David and Douglas Wade, and Susan Wade Warner. They deliver milk to stores, hospitals and schools, and are one of the very few dairies still making home deliveries.

BOTTOM: This type of bottle is fairly common; Samovar Vodka and Virginia Dare Beverages.

TOP: **Tipo Sherry and Lone Star beer.**

CENTER: **There are a lot of beer related collectors who also collect salt and peppers like these Old Milwaukee beer cans. The TWA shakers were probably given out with meals; these are heavier than contemporary plastic and again have dual collectability--to airline collectors as well as S&P collectors.**

BOTTOM: **According to Jo Helmig, a collector from New York, these wonderful "Bud Man" shakers were sold at Busch Gardens in 1970 for $7.95 a pair. They are now worth between $35-55.00. These Coca Cola bottle shakers are unusual because they are ceramic and not glass.**

Animals

This photo shows a pair of Van Tellingen Huggies. Animals are without question the most common form of salt and pepper shakers. In any collection that I have seen or bought animals outnumber any other category unless it is a specialized collection. Again the appeal is reaching farther than just salt and pepper collecting. I have met people who collect elephants, zebras, mice, dogs, cats and even hippopatami! They will add shakers to their collection of animals.

TOP: Cats with sunglasses and umbrellas. Cats with bows to identify the gender.

CENTER: Tall stylized cats marked Napco, Japan. Bisque Siamese cats; very nice quality.

BOTTOM: Holt-Howard cats--these are from the 1950's. The shakers sit in a base which includes a spring holder for cards or paper napkins. These same cats come in full figure.

10

TOP: **Lions and leopards-- bone china--marked "hand- painted" Relco.**

CENTER: **Lions with fur trim from Norcrest Fur- land.**

BOTTOM: **Deco heavy metal Scotties--these are remi- niscent of the Mack Truck bulldog hood orna- ment. The tails unscrew to fill. Two piece Yale bulldog; invisible in this shot, but there is a bright blue band between head and body.**

FROM NORCREST FURLAND

MAY I BE YOUR PAL

TOP: **Monkey in car. Nice pair of Spaniels.**

CENTER: **Cartoon type animals.**

BOTTOM: **The poodle on the pillow is new-- by Sarsaparilla 1983; Choosie and dog- house; according to Irene Thornburg, of Battle Creek, Michi- gan it is difficult to tell which dog in this series goes with which doghouse. Irene gave a speech at the 1989 Salt and Pepper Shaker con- vention in Cleveland, Ohio. Besides "Choosie" the other dogs in the series are named "Sad Sack," "Weary," "Happy," "Grouchy," "Dreamie," and "Shootie."**

TOP: **This set is German and belongs to Charlene Wallace. Another dog in doghouse; this one is "Dreamie."**

CENTER: **This chalkware set is a dachshund meeting his own tail around a stump. It says "There's a new dog in town." Very nice English Bulldogs. (Real breeds of dogs are worth more than the cartoon type and are desirable to dog collectors.)**

BOTTOM: **Boston bull terriers.**

13

TOP: **This set came from the Boothe Museum and was a total surprise to me. I had seen the bone alone and thought it was a one-piece shaker. Here it is part of a vinegar and oil cruet set.**

CENTER: **Stylized zebras--these are very graphic--a deco look.**

BOTTOM: **These shakers are 6" tall. The duck and deer on the left are probably not a pair; they came together in a collection, and one is marked "S" and one "P." Dogs with green collars.**

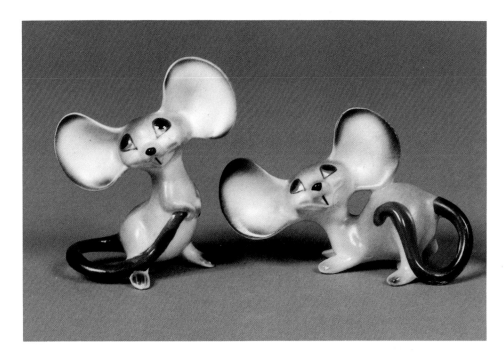

TOP: Dressed mice--animals in people's clothing is a category of collectible that appeals to many. These mice are all dressed up to go out for a stroll with their baby. Golfing animals; I thought these were mice but their noses look like pigs. Anyone's guess!

CENTER: A pair of mice with extraordinary ears--must be related to Dumbo!

BOTTOM: Gray mouse with wedge of cheese.

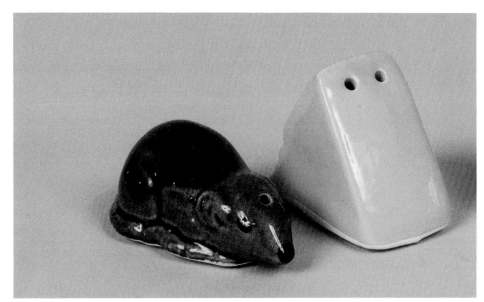

TOP: **Another version of the hare and the tortoise.**

CENTER LEFT: **Rabbit with carrot--very heavy pottery.**

CENTER RIGHT: **These rabbit heads are in the garden which is also a napkin holder. The heads fit through holes.**

BOTTOM: **The new sets made by Sarsaparilla are such good copies that its hard to distinguish them by looks alone. The old ones are heavier than the new and the pottery has more density. The new set here (the rabbit in the middle) is marked 1981. It's very helpful that the date is incised and not just on a paper label.**

TOP: **This mother and baby cow is part of a series; a small piece of florist's clay will hold the baby in place. The bear holding the fish comes in many color combinations; I particularly like the bright blue fish.**

CENTER: **Cartoon type cows; milk cans with cow heads in relief on front.**

BOTTOM: **This is one of the nicest sets of cows I've seen; they belong to Boothe Memorial Park. The only mark on them is PY Japan.**

17

TOP: Buffalo salt and pepper shakers are quite scarce; Steer.

CENTER: A pair of bulls; mother and baby bear--precarious position for baby.

BOTTOM: Small bone china horses. The donkeys have three rhinestones, and may qualify for the ugliest pair contest!

18

TOP: **This is a marvelous set-- the Democratic donkey and the Republican elephant. Imagine them sharing the same dinner table.**

CENTER: **Donkeys carrying jugs; there are many, many variations on this theme.**

BOTTOM: **An oxen pulling a hay wagon on tray. A nice camel carring two shakers; there is a lid missing to the mustard.**

TOP: Lavender giraffes with gold bows. Nondescript donkeys.

CENTER: Both pairs of elephants in this photograph are wonderful. Elephant and circus tent. Elephants dressed in clothes.

BOTTOM: Elephants playing baseball. Two cats on couch.

TOP: **Silly looking elephants. Dapper foxes with top hats and canes.**

CENTER: **Cavorting hippos. Elephants dressed as a trainman and his chamber maid (?).**

BOTTOM: **Two pairs of hippos--charming for the table--especially if you're on a diet.**

21

TOP: **Bone china seals--nice detail. The second pair is luster and gold-- but what are they? Bears? Lambs?**

CENTER: **Frog and accordion-these are old. Unusual alligators--green, white and red.**

BOTTOM: **A one piece alligator--salt and pepper come out at either end. There is a divider inside in the mid- dle. An unusual and very beautiful flamingo and flower set.**

TOP: Rare walrus set-- look at those tusks! Kangaroo with twin babies; the babies are the salt and pepper; the mother is just the holder.

CENTER: An unusual white kangaroo and baby; in this set the baby is one shaker and the mother is the other. Sitting giraffes.

BOTTOM: These are the largest frogs I've ever seen, and I'm not even sure they are salt and pepper shakers; however, sugar shakers don't usually come in pairs. This is one of an average frog shaker that I put in for size comparison.

TOP: **This is another large frog sitting on a crocodile. The set is marked "Sigma." It is very whimsical. The frog, wearing bright orange pants and a brilliant royal blue jacket is a fantastic set. He is carrying tomatoes that exactly match his pants.**

CENTER: **The second candidate for the ugliest pair! These gorillas are humorous to say the least.**

BOTTOM: **Monkey resting on a banana. This monkey with a bowl of bananas on his head has the same face as the other set, and must have been made by the same company.**

TOP: **Monkey hanging from palm tree; this set is old. Vandor made a new set with two monkeys hanging from a palm tree. Monkey playing a bass fiddle--this is also an older set.**

CENTER LEFT: **Pigs playing the accordion.**

CENTER RIGHT : **Dressed cartoon pigs playing leap frog. Mother monkey and baby playing piggyback.**

BOTTOM: **Tiny pigs with bone china flower decoration. Sleeping pigs snuggling.**

25

TOP: These pink pigs are very heavy and look like the German ones but they are not marked. Pig Nodders--these are different from the pair on p.95 in my first book. They are in the same pose but are wearing different clothes. The most common nodders are in a rectangular white base; the figural bases are more scarce, and therefore more expensive.

BOTTOM: These pigs and fish are both signed C. Miller, and were made by the Regal China Company. They are very heavy and are one piece shakers.

TOP: **Pigs with magnets in their noses--WHY? Heavy one piece pig-- shaker at either end.**

CENTER: **More dressed animals. Tiny bears. Cartoon dogs.**

BOTTOM: **Deco dogs--very appealing. Dog dressed as a circus ringmaster by Shafford Pottery. The ball is the other shaker.**

CHILDREN

Everyone loves children's things. Comics and cartoon characters have an almost universal appeal. We all want to believe in fairy tales, and Disneyland and Disney World are as popular with adults as with children. One need just visit any large antique show to see the proliferation of toy dealers. Children's things, whether in the area of salt and pepper shakers, or any other collectible, are here to stay.

TOP: These wonderful chalkware sets are from the 1940's. They are in extremely fine condition, as paint usually peels from chalk. Jack and Jill--Jill with the bucket, and Jack on his head. Little Orphan Annie and Sandy.

CENTER: Goldilocks--by Relco; she is holding a book titled "The Three Bears." This set looks as though it might be from "Alice in Wonderland"; Her cat is beside her, but I can't identify the man. I've made many inquiries at children's libraries, etc., but to no avail. I would appreciate any information.

BOTTOM: Little Bo Peep, another in the Relco series. A charming little couple, nicely crafted.

29

TOP: Little Miss Muffet and the spider. Pinocchio--these are beautifully painted in wonderful colors.

CENTER: Woody and Winnie Woodpecker--1958; Walter Lantz Productions, Inc. Napco, Japan. Two monks--Atchoo (pepper) and Salt of the Earth.

BOTTOM: I've seen many different versions of Humpty Dumpty, but these are the nicest so far. The heads lift out of the one-piece base. Unfortunately for the pigs, this looks more like a butcher than a farmer; Very nice quality--old.

TOP: Mickey Mouse on a plain cylinder--not too imaginative. I saw a fabulous Mickey Mouse condiment set complete with spoon at the Atlantic City Antique Show--It was from the 1930's and marked $1,750.00 The dealer said I could have it for $1,500.00. Probably the most expensive set I've seen. Donald Duck and Ludwig Von Drake designed by Dan Brechner.

CENTER: These two sets look like they were made by the same company at the same time. The pair on the left is marked Robinson Crusoe.

BOTTOM : Rockabye Baby looks like it might be part of the same series as the preceding two pairs. These ducks look like a Walt Disney knock-off.

TOP: **Pluto--another Japanese knock-off not authorized by Disney.**

CENTER AND BOTTOM: **Gnomes--Robin Kinney, an avid collector from Ridgefield, Connecticut, told me that there is a TV program called "David the Gnome." It is a children's program, in which every episode is a lesson in kindness. The gnomes are friendly with all the forest animals--deer, rabbit, fox, etc. and there is a salt and pepper shaker for each. The book, *The Gnomes* has text by Wil Huygen, and illustrations by Rien Poortvliet. It was originally published under the title "*Leven en Werken van de Kabouter*" in 1976 by Unieboek B.V./Van Hlokema & Warendorf, the Netherlands. The English translation was published in New York by Harry N. Abrams, Inc. in 1977. The shakers are marked "Made in Japan, QQ, 1979, Uniebok, B.V. and were imported by the Quon Quon Company. I have the Abrams book, and the shakers are very true to the illustrations.**

32

TOP: There are many different versions of Humpty Dumpty and the cow that jumped over the moon. Here are two more.

CENTER: These three sets belong to the same series and were designed by the same company. Cow and moon, Puss in Boots, and the cat and the fiddle.

BOTTOM: Garfield and Odie--not very old, but very popular.

TOP: **Teddy bear and doll.**

BOTTOM: **Vandor has re-issued this Popeye and Olive Oyl from the same mold as the 1980 set. The set with Popeye and Swee' Pea in the boat has not been re-issued. Vandor is the importer; the shakers are made in Japan. These shakers are licensed by King Feature Syndicates (KFS)-- owned by the Hearst Corporation; Vandor works with their artists.**

Condiment Sets

Condiment sets consist of a container for salt, pepper, and mustard. In England they are called cruets. This set was given to a friend of mine who was tutoring Russian immigrants...The set cost 12 rubles in Russia. Since this is not easily translatable into dollars, the woman told my friend that she earned 100 rubles a month making this quite an expensive set. They came from a village near Leningrad called Gjel. The shakers, of course, are reminiscent of the Matreshka sets where one fits in another--in another--in another...

TOP: **This is a spectacular set--the claws are the salt and pepper, the body is the mustard, and the tail is the handle attached to the tray.**

CENTER: **These luster houses are by Noritake China. The mark is a red M.**

BOTTOM: **The black woman with the three pumpkins is a set I bought in England. The lid to the mustard is missing. This is another charming Old World set that seems related to the Rockabye baby and Robinson Crusoe sets shown earlier. The sheep are the shakers; the tree stump is the mustard.**

TOP: **Both of these sets are from England. They are luster-ware with transfers of different resorts. These are used on many different china souvenir items, and are similar to postcard scenes.**

CENTER: **These two sets also traveled with me from England--unfortunately the tiny spoons often get broken. The dog set says "A present from Gt. Yarmouth."**

BOTTOM: **This kangaroo set is unique--the two babies are the salt and pepper, and the baby in the mother's pouch is the lid for the mustard.**

TOP: Another souvenir from England...the boat says "A present from Brighton." This set is luster, and does have the spoon (and smoke!). Made in Germany. The Indian condiment set is great. The drum is for mustard.

CENTER: Three windmills on a tray--made in Japan. Donkey and cart--also Japanese.

BOTTOM: This lovely little gold and white china set came in this charming old box.

TOP: **The train set has great colors and is charming.**

CENTER: **Baseball set. The spoon for the mustard is in the shape of a bat.**

BOTTOM: **Yellow chicken set by Noritake...missing an oval tray.**

TOP: **This set of pagodas looks as though it should have a tray.**

BOTTOM: **One of my all-time favorites: I've had several sets of girls and boys from this time period--all with orange hats and a deco look. I've never seen them with a protrusion on the bottom to fit into the holes cut in the trunk. The gladstone bag, or valise is the mustard, and the spoon is bright yellow.**

TOP: **This is a Belisha beacon--the pedestrian crossing light invented by Hore-Belisha in 1934. He was a member of the British Parliament and Minister of Transport. The crosswalk at the flashing beacon has black lines and is called a Zebra. There were many other objects depicting the Belisha beacon as well as the salt and pepper shakers.**

RIGHT: **I also took a photograph of a real Belisha beacon right outside the shop where I bought the objects; they are all over London, and I had never noticed one before!**

BOTTOM: **Here is an hour glass, pencil, ashtray and match holder, a card game similar to Rummy to teach children safety at crossing, and a trump marker for Bridge.**

Feathers and Fins

This is an old print I picked up in an antique shop in Middlebury, Vermont. It made a great background for the red and white salt and pepper shakers. These are made in Japan, quite common.

TOP: **These are unusually large swans--5½x4½".**

CENTER: **Pink birds with gold trim--long tails.**

BOTTOM: **Stylized birds--wonderful colors. Large red birds.**

TOP: **Orange and green birds marked Staffordshire, England. Tails are attached to corks and come out for re-filling. Luster-swans-beautifully colored, probably were once on a tray.**

CENTER: **Baby penguins on skates--penguins are very collectible. Magpies all dressed up.**

BOTTOM: **Pelicans. Ostrich and baby--not many of these around.**

TOP: **An assortment of small exotic birds--some luster.**

CENTER: **Pheasants on a basket--these same bright colored green and yellow sets with flowers on basket or tray have been found with several other animals (see Book II-p.15). Realistically colored ducks.**

BOTTOM: **Owls on a tray. Cartoon birds.**

TOP: **Classic red and white chickens. Very nice detail on these Barred Plymouth Rock chickens.**

CENTER: **Mother bird is attached to tray and the babies are the salt and pepper shakers.**

BOTTOM: **Cartoon birds and ducks.**

TOP: **Small bone china swans. Powder puff pigeons.**

CENTER: **Bright red cartoon octopuses. Star fish.**

BOTTOM: **Creel of fish from Portugal--heavy, nice quality. Hanging fish on stand.**

TOP: **Colorful, but unrealistic fish.**

CENTER ABOVE: **Real clams made into shakers. Ceramic clams.**

CENTER BELOW: **I'm not sure what these are-- someone suggested that they are the top view of a conch shell-- but I'm dubious. Red striped fish.**

BOTTOM: **Rainbow trout. Swordfish, marked San Diego. Calif.**

Food

This 1940's style tablecloth goes well with the large bright fruit and vegetable shakers that were popular then. Food is a natural for an accessory that goes on the table. A separate and delightful category of food shakers is that of fruit and vegetable people. These are very comic and are fun to collect; there are so many different ones available.

TOP: **These cupcakes look good enough to eat!**

CENTER: **Corn on the cob; nice detail-- repeated on tray. These watermelons look like papier maché, but they are ceramic.**

BOTTOM: **Watermelons and apples. Both sets are realistically painted.**

TOP: These, I think, are the most charming type of all the fruit and vegetable people. The heads, with eyes, nose and mouth, are also given bodies. Often the arms and feet are in a comic position. These are pumpkins and squash.

CENTER: Mushroom people. Cucumber people--these have the same "gingerbread" trim that is often found on old Christmas sets. I believe they are older, 1930-40.

BOTTOM: Red peppers and peanuts--the expressions on their faces are wonderful.

51

TOP: Lettuce and celery people.

CENTER: Besides their silly faces, these shakers have googly eyes that move!

BOTTOM: More full figure vegetable and fruit heads.

TOP: **These are just heads with faces; very cheerful!**

CENTER: **Onion heads on a tray. Tomato heads. Four peas in a pod on a tray; the two center ones have faces.**

BOTTOM: **Full figure people doing people things. The banana and pineapple heads are boxing; the carrot and pea head are doing housework. There are figures like these painting, playing musical instruments, and playing sports.**

TOP: The orange is different; the hat comes off and is one shaker; the orange is the other. The strawberries have a ceramic base which unscrews.

CENTER: Corn People--5" tall. Cabbage girls; these have realistic female faces.

BOTTOM: Two wonderful sets of peas. The set on the left has a very nicely detailed tray. The standing pea stands in a wire frame with hands attached to the frame. He stands over the salt, lying at his feet.

Going Places

The wooden ship in this photograph is one of the nicest wooden sets I've seen. It is very sleek. Similar ships with smokestacks as the salt and pepper shakers are found in chrome, plastic and ceramic. The cover illustration on the book was done by my son, Steven Guarnaccia, and the book was published by St. Martin's Press.

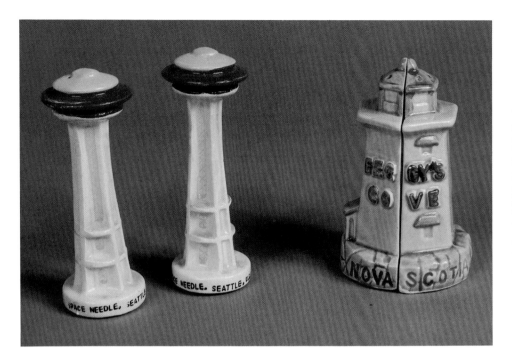

TOP: Space Needle, Seattle, Washington. I've had these in pot metal; these are china. Peggy's Cove, Nova Scotia--the Light House. This is one of the most visited and one of the most photographed spots in Canada.

CENTER: The Ozarks... both jugs have a Mammy and a Pappy smoking a pipe.

BOTTOM: This group really represents going places! Two pairs of flying saucers-the green ones are by Coventry Ware Inc., 1950. A rocket ship and a character carrying a suitcase that says "To Mars." He has string hair, and the set is marked Enesco.

56

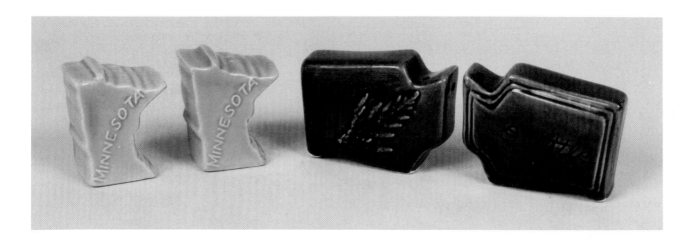

TOP: **Two sets of states. Minnesota with raised lettering is by Milford Pottery. The dark green set says Seattle, Washington, but has no other mark or identification.**

CENTER ABOVE: **Another pair of states; this is completely different as the two shakers make one state. New Hampshire...metal with various tourist attractions in relief, and in colors: Old Man of the Mountain. The Flume, Crawford Notch, Franconia Aerial Tramway, Mt. Sunapee, etc...These were made in Japan, and imported by Parksmith, NYC.**

CENTER BELOW: **USS Alabama pictured on a china cylinder. Another state--Missouri and a mule. This is not Parkcraft. The bottom of the state is indented and has a regular cork. This indentation requires a three part mold. The Parkcraft States, flat on the bottom, only needed a two part mold--their holes must be covered with tape.**

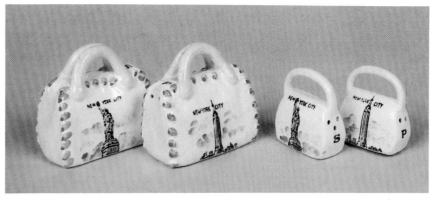

BOTTOM: **Suitcases and pocketbooks--New York City. Both sets picture the Empire State Building and the Statue of Liberty.**

TOP: **Aquarena, San Marcos, Texas--this view of the canal looks hand painted.**

CENTER: **1964 World's Fair--all metal--silver and gold color.**

BOTTOM: **"Spud" potato heads from Idaho. Wood golf balls on tees. The sticker says NYC. Teddy bears bought on the Pennsylvania Turnpike.**

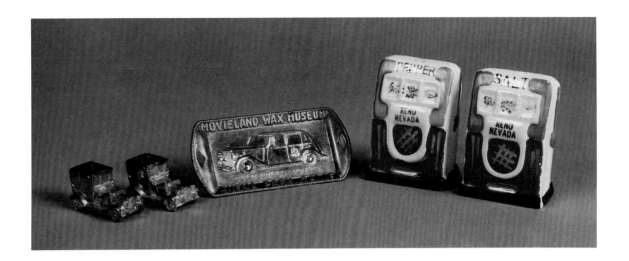

TOP: **Movieland Wax Museum--tray with two cars; the car on the metal tray is a gold Rolls Royce, and so are the shakers. Slot machines from Reno, Nevada-ceramic.**

CENTER ABOVE: **Air flow trailer and streamline car--the 1950's. Pyramid and camel--a long way to go in a trailer!**

CENTER BELOW: **Chalkware... these are in amazingly good condition, considering their age. They say "U.S.S. Arizona, Dec. 7, 1941" and on the other "Remember Pearl Harbor." Chalkware tanks--also in good condition, but not marked.**

BOTTOM: **These ceramic racing cars with metal wheels come in many different colors and have different stickers on them representing different car makes. The metal airplanes are very nicely crafted; they are heavy and stand at a nice angle.**

Holidays

These sets are really fun to use at appropriate holidays and add to the table decor. I have corresponded with a caterer who incorporates seasonal shakers into her table settings. Last year I made a gingerbread house for Christmas and had Santa Claus, snowmen and Christmas tree shakers surrounding it. The Christmas card pictured here was illustrated by my son, and printed in Hong Kong by the Dickens Company, N.Y.

TOP: Halloween--pumpkins wearing hats. Witches--these are not old--1980--but great fun!

CENTER: Mother's Day--a really nice gift for a collecting Mom.

BOTTOM: Wedding--this ring and wedding license is new. I've included it here as it would make a nice addition tucked into the bow of a wedding or shower gift. This is a copy of the old set which was a miniature.

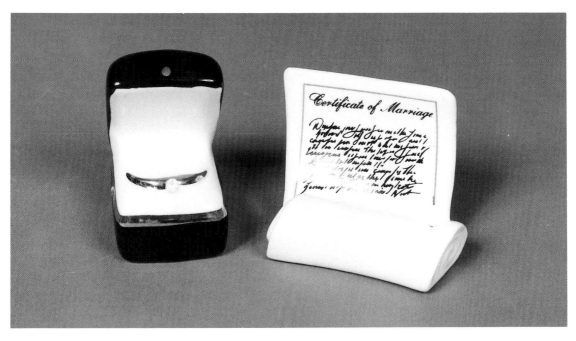

TOP: There are many couples of all nationalities that are "bench sitters," and come with a wooden bench. I gave this bride and groom to my nephew and his fiancée when they became engaged.

CENTER: These two sets are both quite old; the brides are wearing real net dresses. The one of the brass altar is marked "Dan Brechner and Co."

BOTTOM: These wedding bells are 46 years old and still have the original satin bows on them. They may have been favors at each table at the wedding. The other two pairs came in the same collection, and obviously belonged to the same couple.

TOP: **These anniversary hearts are bone china trimmed in gold.**

CENTER: **A nice shiny red heart for Valentine's Day.**

BOTTOM: **Pilgrim hats--to grace a Thanksgiving table.**

TOP: **Stylized Pilgrim man and woman.**

CENTER: **There are probably dozens of different turkeys for the Thanksgiving table, but these are exceptionally nice.**

BOTTOM: **Needless to say, Christmas sets far outnumber those for any other holiday. This Santa sitting atop a pile of packages has a magnet in his bottom. The set is by Holt-Howard. Mr. and Mrs. Santa sitting on a bench.**

64

TOP: A nice Mr. and Mrs. Santa with a distinctive turquoise trim.

CENTER: This Santa and Christmas tree is quite heavy and seems older than most-- possibly 1940's. It is marked Murray Kreiss & Co.

BOTTOM: Christmas pigs by Kreiss. Santa and reindeer-- this set is unusual.

TOP: **Mr. and Mrs. Santa sitting in their rockers talking over the events of the day.**

BOTTOM: **A nice old pair of Santas with lots of gingerbread trim and bright blue eyes.**

TOP: **This pair also has the old gingerbread trim.**

BOTTOM: **A sweet little church and priest. A pair of angels--lovely faces.**

67

Hodgepodge

This is a miscellaneous collection, consisting of plastic, wood and metal sets. I didn't have enough in any of these categories to warrant devoting a whole section to each. The wood chickens are from Russia. These cost two rubles and are considered expensive tourist items. They came from Central Russia: Near Moscow is a ring of small towns called "the gold ring" where many artisans work.

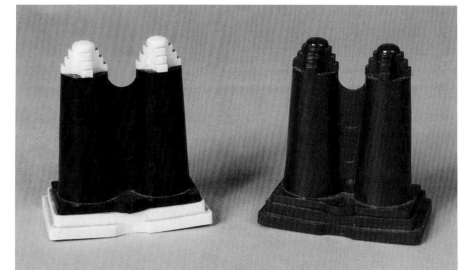

TOP: Both of these sets are very architectural. They are made of carvanite and there is a button on the bottom of each. When pushed the salt and pepper flows.

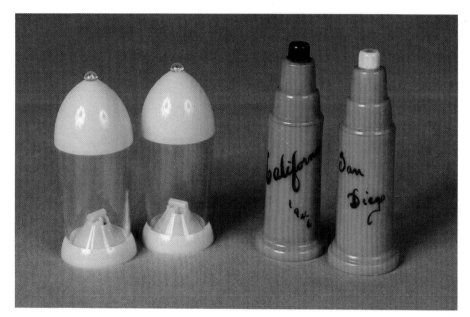

CENTER: There are innumerable rockets and other plastic shakers of this type.

BOTTOM: A rubber lily pad with two plastic flowers and a tiny metal frog. The owls are self-explanatory.

TOP: The more common toaster is chrome. There are plastic ones like this in various colors. When the lever is pushed down the toast pops.

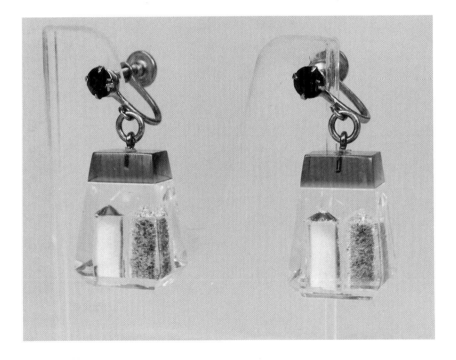

CENTER: These Lucite earrings are the only ones I have ever seen. They were in a collection that I purchased; most of the shakers were from the 1940's and 1950's. I love these, wear them often, and they are not for sale.

BOTTOM: These Bakelite shakers are very collectible; the red are the most desirable.

TOP: **Ball canning jars complete with rubber sealing rings. Another plastic pair is this set of green parakeets on a branch. I have seen these in yellow on a white branch; this green set is more unusual.**

CENTER: **"Please pass the salt" these wind-up salt and pepper will march down the table for you!**

BOTTOM: **For some reason I find wood shakers difficult to sell. These, however, are particularly nice. The horse drawn wagon is a souvenir of Westport, Connecticut, the town next to mine. Deco ship has smokestack shakers.**

TOP: **Axe & stump. Deer in wood shakers.**

CENTER: **These wooden shakers are decorated in bright enamel.**

BOTTOM: **Wooden windmills and Vikings from Denmark.**

TOP: **Clocks made of wood and walnut birds with chenille tails.**

BOTTOM: **The glass shaker on the right is a standard restaurant item. I had it photographed to show the scale of the shaker on the left from Think Big in New York City. It makes a great container for jelly beans or flowers.**

CENTER: **Silver colored metal pigs. These are heavy and very unusual. Gold metal seals.**

TOP: **Glass paint pots with plastic lids on a metal palette.**

CENTER ABOVE: **Two pairs of Goebel sets. Chimney sweeps and dogs.**

CENTER BELOW: **The salt and pepper shakers are the jugs that these donkeys are carrying.**

BOTTOM: **Football and helmet.**

TOP: **Totem poles on a tray.**

CENTER: **Here's a real hodge podge! Seltzer bottles and legs.**

BOTTOM: **Tiny chefs. Suitcase and valise.**

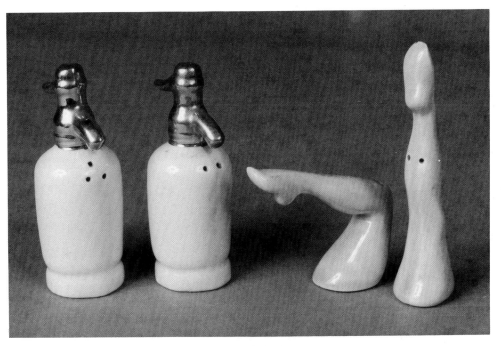

Household Objects

This photo consists of some of the innumerable household objects that have been depicted in the form of shakers. There are several collectors who decorate doll houses with salt and pepper shaker furniture and accessories.

TOP: Faucets are in white china with colored taps. Red and green ceramic telephone is very unusual. The receiver is one shaker and the base the other.

CENTER: Another telephone not as finely detailed. Record player and television.

BOTTOM: This black telephone is the more common but very finely crafted. It is probably from the 1940's. Paint bucket and brush. Sets that have two different shakers are often called Go-Withs.

TOP LEFT: **Easy chair and ottoman-another Go-With.**

TOP RIGHT: **Anthropomorphic tea and coffee pots.**

CENTER: **White china coffee and tea pots decorated with red cherries.**

BOTTOM: **Watering cans with garden poem.**

THE KISS OF THE SUN FOR PARDON
THE SONG OF THE BIRD FOR MIRTH
ONE IS NEARER GOD'S HEART IN
A GARDEN
THAN ANYWHERE
ELSE ON EARTH

TOP AND CENTER:
Two-sided creamer and sugar-Happy and Sad.

BOTTOM: **An exceptionally nice set of binoculars with case trimmed in gold.**

TOP: Two more sets of watering cans.

CENTER: Salt and pepper books and rolling pin and scoop.

BOTTOM: Candlesticks come in many shapes and sizes.

TOP: Egg cup people with egg-shaped salt and peppers. These also appeal to egg cup collectors.

CENTER: White ceramic stove and refrigerator vintage 1940's.

BOTTOM: Clothes hanging on ceramic hangers. I wonder if there are many variations on these sets. They are charming.

TOP: **Baby shoes look bronze but are ceramic.**

CENTER: **These houses are identical but are photographed to show back and front.**

BOTTOM: **Two more pairs of Go-withs-baseball and glove, thermos and lunchbox.**

Japanese Luster

Most of the luster sets are from the 1920's and 1930's and are Deco in design. Metallic oxides were used with the glazes to produce a lustrous effect. Many of these sets are from my personal collection. They are so hard to find that I am willing to include singles. This photo shows a Noritake condiment set on tray and a single figure.

TOP: The center figure is a powdered sugar shaker marked Noritake. Salt and pepper shakers with the cloche hats and style of dress are from the same time period but are not marked Noritake (1920's).

CENTER: Lusterware comes in peach, blue, greens and orange.

BOTTOM: Deco figures.

TOP: Three singles. Tiny pair has googly eyes.

CENTER: Roly-poly blue luster harlequins. Small lady with spit curls is from the 1920's.

BOTTOM: Luster clowns.

TOP: **1920's couple in open roadster. Note the lady driver (the steering wheel is attached to her hand).**

CENTER ABOVE: **Condiment set has large bird as the mustard. Set of luster bird shakers in holder.**

CENTER BELOW: **More birds-- open salts, birds in holder, funny-billed birds.**

BOTTOM: **Luster birds in holders. Lady with wheel-barrow.**

TOP: **Galleons.**

BOTTOM: **Dogs in tray. Tiny birds.**

CENTER: **Flowers in tray. Washington Monument unusual in luster.**

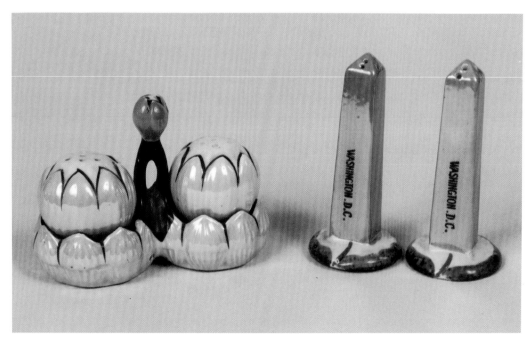

Miniatures

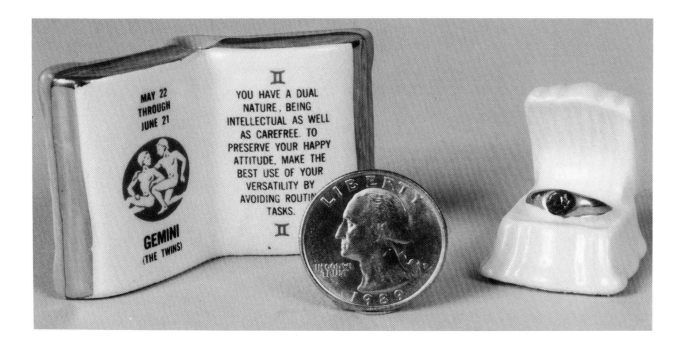

Most miniatures were made to be collected not used. They have tiny holes too small for a cork, and wouldn't hold enough to have any practical value. One of the foremost producers of miniatures was Arcadia Ceramics Inc., Arcadia, California. Their shakers were packaged in a plastic bubble pack. In the photo there is a set consisting of a horoscope book and a ring in jeweller's box. This is probably not the correct match as June's birthstone is a pearl, and there must be 11 more sets: one for each zodiac sign. The quarter is to show relative size.

TOP: Sausage and eggs. Pancakes and syrup (note knife & fork).

CENTER: Chocolate candies in paper wrap (real paper). Coffee pot with cup & saucer.

BOTTOM: Dust pan and whisk broom. Box of chocolate & flowers.

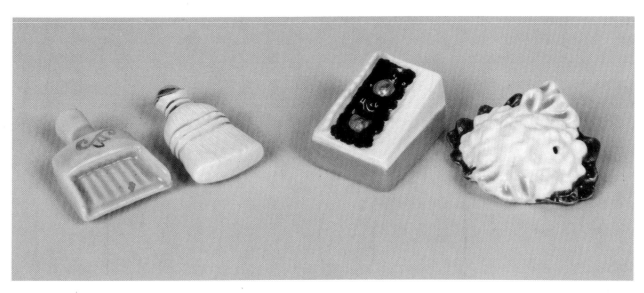

TOP: Garden gate and garden hat.

CENTER: Mouse and mousetrap. Dog and dog food.

BOTTOM: Violin and accordian. Purse and pocket watch.

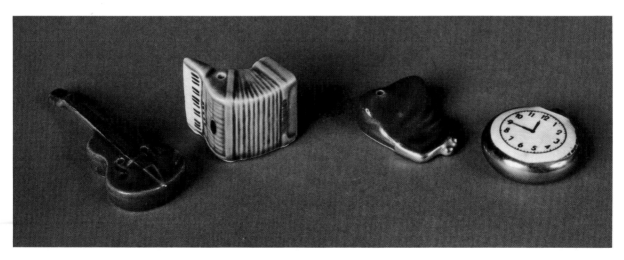

TOP: Sir George and dragon. Aladdin on flying carpet and lamp.

CENTER: Bathtub and kettle. Outhouses with antenna.

BOTTOM: Sherlock Holmes' hat and pipe and book with magnifing glass. Diary and love letters.

TOP: Ice cream maker and ice cream. Cake and slice comes in many flavors; this one is lemon.

CENTER: Pipe and slippers. Shaving brush and mug.

BOTTOM: Roller skates. Ice skates and sled.

TOP: **Body buried in sand with beach umbrella. Oyster with pearl and lobster.**

CENTER: **Cowboy boots. Fishing creel and catch.**

BOTTOM: **Safe and safe-cracking tools. Stop sign and car.**

93

TOP: **Toys: ball, jack-in-a-box, rocking horse, buggy, drum and trumpet (these are not paired).**

CENTER: **Orange and gourd. Barbecue and picnic table.**

BOTTOM: **Telescope and Saturn. Graduation cap and diploma.**

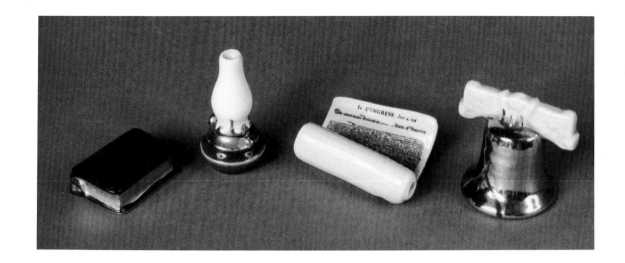

TOP: **Book and hurricane lamp. Liberty Bell and Declaration of Independence.**

CENTER: **Pair of bride's cookbooks.**

BOTTOM: **Oversized mini-snowman and sled; laundry tub and soap.**

People

One of the largest categories to be found in salt and pepper shakers is people. Many nationalities are represented, as well as, many occupations. In addition there are cartoon and unrealistic types. There is overlapping, of course, with children, famous people, etc. This is an old Chinese checkerboard with six different oriental sets.

TOP LEFT: **Oriental boy nicely detailed carrying the shakers on his back.**

TOP RIGHT: **Oriental boy and pagoda on boat.**

BOTTOM: **Oriental Good Luck figures. Beautifully designed Japanese women.**

97

TOP: **Two pairs; same mold with a different finish. One is black/white/gold and the other is brightly colored.**

CENTER: **This is a most unusual set. A lovely metal figure--the shakers fit in a metal ring and are made of Bakelite.**

BOTTOM: **Hawaiian girls.**

98

TOP: **Royal Canadian Mounted Police. Hawaiian couple.**

CENTER: **Two Dutch couples from Delft, Holland.**

BOTTOM: **Two children on green ceramic bench. Dutch couple in wooden shoes.**

99

TOP: **Scottish couple 6½" tall. Small Scottish couple 3".**

CENTER: **Eskimo couple; paper sticker says 1959 Alaska. Cartoon type Eskimos marked Canada.**

BOTTOM: **Cactus and Mexican. American Indian and tepee.**

TOP: Indian and tepee. Pilgrim couple.

CENTER: This couple looks Tyrolean-but the inscription says "Nuestra Señora de Los Angeles" (Our Lady of the Angels).

BOTTOM: These are lovely old sets. The shakers lift out of the wagons.

TOP: **Kitchen witches.**

CENTER LEFT: **Baby boxers. A man and woman doing push-ups.**

CENTER RIGHT: **This delightful boy has his hands full! His mate is in** *Salt & Pepper Shakers II,* **page 144.**

BOTTOM: **Whimsical elves. Women with crooked smiles.**

TOP: Baby heads. Devils holding metal tridents.

CENTER: Graduates. What's Hers is Hers and What's His is Hers.

BOTTOM: Holt-Howard children. Babies with flowered hats.

TOP: **Two charming young couples.**

CENTER: **Holt-Howard little girls--stickers say New York Thruway. Another charming couple. He is holding a trowel and she is holding an apple.**

BOTTOM: **Civil War babies. Tall (6½") Royal couple. R.C.M.P. (wood).**

104

TOP: **Bride and Groom.**

BOTTOM: **Two-sided bride and groom--as a young couple and as an old couple.**

TOP: **Grandparents in rockers--she's knitting and he's smoking a pipe. This picture is of two sets. Each person and each rocker is a shaker.**

CENTER: **Three girls on a tray. The middle one is a dinner bell.**

BOTTOM: **Golfer on tray with over-sized golf ball. The tray is made up of four golf clubs. By Goebel.**

106

TOP: Green clown is one shaker and the yellow ball is the other. The clowns hand fits into a hole in the ball. Red and white clown is holding a dog dressed in identical outfit on his lap.

CENTER: Clowns by C. Miller made by Regal China Company.

BOTTOM: Wonderful fat chefs by Fitz & Floyd.

TOP: Fireman boy and girl--these are the ones from 1960. English Bobbies.

CENTER: These monks were made by Twin Winton. I had the cookie jar to match. The cookie jar was marked San Juan, California USA, and said "Thou shalt not steal!" across the bottom.

BOTTOM: On the left a pair of pirates, one with a wooden leg. Sea captains with pipes--a popular subject for shakers.

TOP: **A comic pair of sailors with binoculars.**

CENTER: **Friars with a full head of hair. This is an unusual pair--a nun and a monk.**

BOTTOM **Clown firemen. Lion tamer and lion--a meek looking cat!**

109

TOP: This is another cowboy and hat--he looks Mexican. Trish Claar found patents to this set--Rossware, 1942, by H.L. Ross.

CENTER: A very old style GE refrigerator and chef. Two chefs--they look French but came from New Jersey.

BOTTOM: A chef and his removable hat--each is a shaker. These heads with eyeglasses and pipe are the same faces as a full figured pair in *Collector's Encyclopedia of Figural & Novelty Salt & Pepper Shakers, Vol. ll* by Melva Davern.

TOP: **John F. Kennedy in his famous rocking chair. The set on the left with brown hair, is the original, and has much finer detail.**

CENTER: **This set is one of my all-time favorites. The head is one shaker, and it rests on the collar of the jacket.**

BOTTOM: **A version of Laurel and Hardy--this one without a tray. They are not as well crafted or painted. A pair of frolicking clowns.**

111

TOP: **These egg cups are handy--the hats are the shakers.**

BOTTOM: **This set was a really exciting find. It is designed like the Beswick china set in my first book (p. 102) but is of a very different material and coloration. It is a composition type material, and quite a dark brown. The set was made in Greece--the writing on the box is all in Greek, and even the names of Laurel and Hardy. (Which of course, I can't understand!!)**

TOP: Green faced (and footed) monsters--are these the men in the white coats coming to take us away? Skull and hand.

BOTTOM: A pair of weird monsters.

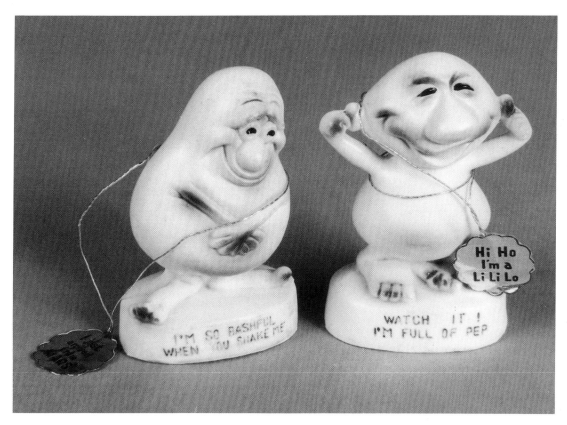

Series

This photo was a work of tremendous concentration and difficulty for me. I know that small children can cut out paper dolls, but that has nothing to do with it. I must have done about ten sets before I figured out how to keep them attached. The salt and peppers in this series are the black and white metal Pennsylvania Dutch so popular with collectors. Many of them are good scale for dollhouses. They range in price depending on scarcity and condition.

TOP: **Famous people series by Parkcraft. We were so lucky to meet the Ahrolds, founders of the Parkcraft Company at the 1988 convention in Michigan. They first started manufacturing the 50 United States. That series was featured in my last book. They then made the Famous Cities set (18), the Famous People series (7), Nursery Rhymes (12), Days of the Week (7), and the Twelve Months of the Year. The Nursery Rhymes and the Days of the Week were made in Japan; the other series were made by the Taneycomo Ceramic Factory of Hollister, Missouri. Heather House in Burlington, Iowa is the name of the mail order company that distributed all of these wonderful sets up to the 1970's. Benjamin Franklin, Charles Lindbergh, and Buffalo Bill are shown here paired with plaques containing biographical data.**

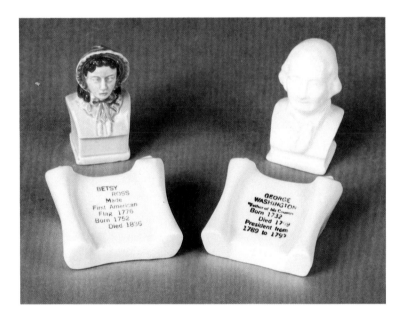

CENTER: **Betsy Ross and George Washington.**

BOTTOM: **Christopher Columbus and Will Rogers.**

115

TOP: **Famous Cities series. For the symbols to go with each foreign city, Bob Ahrold wrote to the foreign embassies in Washington, D.C. for suggestions. For the symbols for each state he wrote to all of the governors. Chicago, the Windy City, and the Wrigley Building. Springfield, Illinois, the birthplace of Lincoln.**

CENTER: **Philadelphia and the Liberty Bell. Washington, D.C. and the Washington Monument.**

BOTTOM: **Hannibal, Missouri and Tom Sawyer. Havana, Cuba, "the tourist city" and Cigar.**

116

TOP: **Rio de Janeiro, Brazil, and a bag of sugar. Honolulu and ukelele.**

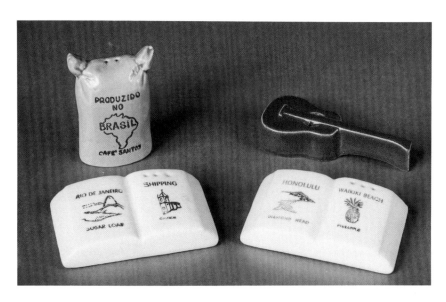

CENTER: **Killarney, Ireland, and a bright green Shamrock. Amsterdam and a "wooden" shoe.**

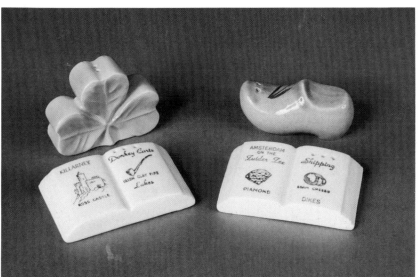

BOTTOM: **Toronto, Canada and a Maple Leaf. London, England and Crown.**

TOP: **Agra, India and the Taj Mahal (not related to Trump's). Tokyo and a colorful Pagoda.**

CENTER: **Paris and the Eiffel Tower. Venice, Italy and a Gondola.**

BOTTOM: **Another wonderful Parkcraft series--the 12 months of the year; January and snowman; February and heart.**

TOP: **March and shamrock with Irish pipe. April with an Easter egg.**

CENTER: **May and basket of flowers. June and a wedding cake.**

BOTTOM: **July with a fire-cracker. August with a bathing beauty.**

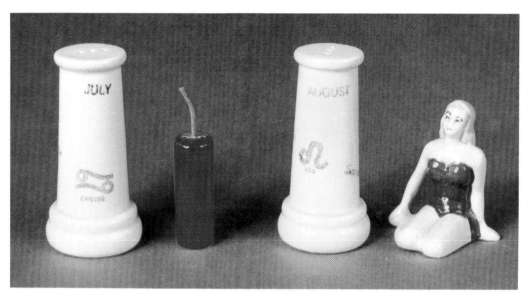

TOP: September and a pile of school books. October and a pumpkin.

CENTER ABOVE: November and a pilgrim's hat. December and a gift.

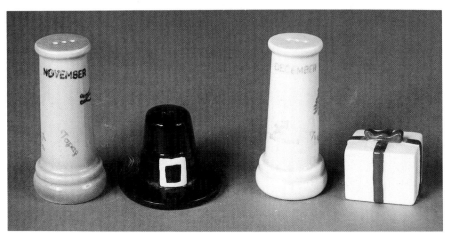

CENTER BELOW: Days of the Week series. These are also by Parkcraft. Monday--wash day; a cake of soap and wash tub. Tuesday--ironing; a laundry basket and iron. Wednesday--mending--a spool of thread and a sewing basket.

BOTTOM: Thursday-visiting day. Friday-cleaning day.

TOP: **Saturday-baking day. Sunday-church.**

CENTER: **Nursery Rhyme sets; these are also by Parkcraft, but these are miniature in size and are made of bone china. Little Boy Blue and cow. Mary Had a Little Lamb.**

BOTTOM: **Old King Cole and his fiddlers three. Little Jack Horner.**

121

TOP: **The Old Woman who lived in a Shoe. Jack and Jill.**

CENTER: **The cow jumping over the moon and the cat & fiddle. Humpty Dumpty.**

BOTTOM: **Little Miss Muffet and tuffet. Little Bo-Peep and sheep (missing: Red Riding Hood and wolf and Peter and pumpkin).**

TOP: Van Tellingen Peek-a-Boo set designed by Ruth Van Tellingen Bendel, and made by the Regal China Corporation. There is a large and small set in this design. They are not huggers as are the series in the *Collector's Encyclopedia of Figural & Novelty Salt & Pepper Shakers, Vol. ll* by Melva Davern. I'm including them here only because she didn't have a pair to show at the time of her book's publication.

CENTER: This set of nuns is a series I have seen only once. They are charming and comical at the same time. Six of them are playing musical instruments, and six are involved in sports. Since I see so many collections and so many pairs of shakers and have never come across these but once, I would classify these as scarce and price them accordingly. They are 6" tall. Bisque finish nun with accordion. Nun with Bongo drum. Nun playing mandolin.

BOTTOM: Nun playing trumpet. Nun with guitar. Nun playing saxaphone.

123

TOP: Nun with catcher's mitt. Nun and soccer ball--she seems to be kicking the ball. Nun with tennis racquet.

BOTTOM: These sports figures are great because in each one she is in the proper stance...Nun playing golf. Nun with ping pong paddle. Nun bowling.

The following photographs of series were sent to me by Irene Thornburg, of Battle Creek, Michigan. They were from a presentation given by her at the 1989 Salt and Pepper Shaker Convention in Cleveland, Ohio. Some of the shakers are from the collection of Joanne Rose of Coldwater, Michigan.

TOP: **Fruit and vegetables doing various 'people' things. Cleaning, painting, and playing music.**

BOTTOM: **Sweethearts of All Nations series by Napco. These were made from 1956-1957. They show a male and female in native costume. When they are placed close together and facing each other they look as though they are kissing. The first six pairs in the series are marked S1286/1 or just 1286/1. They are all 3½" tall. First set: Sweden, Spain, Switzerland, Germany, Holland and Italy.**

TOP: **The second set in the series is marked S1286/2. This second series consists of sets depicting Scotland, India, Alaska, U.S.A., American India, and China.**

BOTTOM: **The last six sets in this Sweetheart series are stamped s1286/3. They are Ireland, Poland, France (man only), Japan, Mexico, and Russia.**

TOP: **The flower of the month girls were made by Napco. Stamped on the bottom of the set is the month and 1C3025. Shown in this photo are January, March, April, June, July, August, September, October, and December.**

BOTTOM: **Office articles used as heads on people bodies. These are similar to the fruit and vegetables people, but are much harder to find. They are marked PY-Japan, and are 3" tall. Shown here are: ink blotters, clocks, cashboxes and typewriters. These are all wearing pants. Dressed in skirts are adding machines, tubes of glue, telephones, and ink bottles. Any suggestions as to the gender difference?**

127

TOP: **Animals driving cars; the steering wheels are attached to the animal, and the car is the other shaker. The cars and animals are probably interchangeable.**

BOTTOM: **Another series where the parts are interchangeable. Each doghouse has a name, but it's almost impossible to determine which dog goes with which house. Shown are Choosie, Sad Sack, Weary, Happy, Grouchie, Dreamie, and Snootie.**

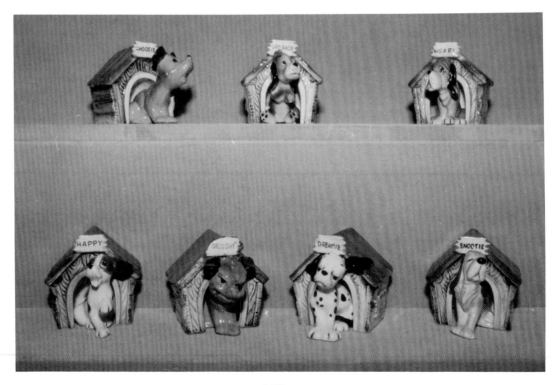

Tomorrow's Collectibles

Salt and Pepper Shakers certainly show trends in style and fashion. If you want to know what's "in," just look for this year's salt and pepper shakers. Last year, 1989, "country" was in and Vandor came out with a wonderful series of black and white cows. This year the Southwest is prevalent in fashion design, in china, linens, and furniture. There are great new shakers in the shape of cactus, guns and holsters, and vultures. 1989 was the 50th anniversary of "The Wizard of Oz," and Clay Art in California has just issued two wonderful sets depicting the characters in that classic story, I wonder if the two baby sets put out by Sarsaparilla have anything to do with the current "baby boom?" This photo shows two sets of Western salt and pepper shakers against a background of real cacti (Courtesy of Mrs. Jean Kass of Fairfield, Connecticut.)

TOP: **Cactus and skull by Vandor.**

CENTER: **Cactus and Vulture.**

BOTTOM: **Two cacti in ceramic pots set on a tray of stones (Vandor). Gun and holster.**

TOP: Two monkeys hanging from a coconut tree. Rattlesnake nodder in Southwestern colors.

CENTER: Bellhop and suitcase--very similar to old Goebel set on the cover of my first book-but in that set each suitcase was a shaker; in this new set, the bellhop is one shaker and the suitcase the other. Gas pump and attendant.

BOTTOM: Giraffes with twisted necks. (Sarsaparilla). Toucans.

TOP: **Tennis balls in metal holder. Soccer balls in holder with ceramic leg.**

CENTER: **Stork and baby. Sarsaparilla has been reproducing some of the old designs; fortunately they are dated in incised print so that no one should be confused. The newer ones also tend to be lighter in weight.**

BOTTOM: **Lying down baby and baby nodder (Sarsaparilla). Comb and brush set.**

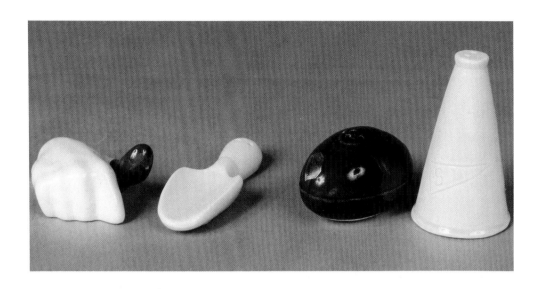

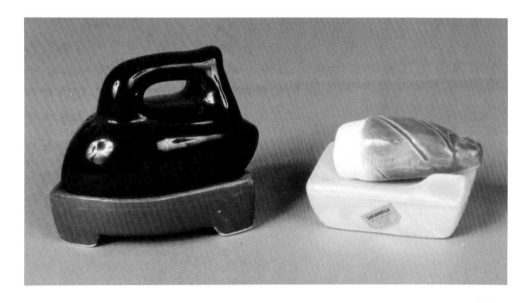

TOP: Trowel and green thumb. Football and megaphone.

CENTER: Sarsaparilla Deco designs also made a group of "go-withs." Iron on stand. Cigar in ashtray.

BOTTOM: Pen and pencil. Two piece television set with paper picture of the Beatles.

TOP: **Some more nostalgia--this time by Vandor. Except for licensed material, such as the Popeye set, most of the Vandor designs are done by Marilyn and Gary Pelzman. Two piece chrome-look jukebox--the kind on the wall in the old diners. Deco chrome-look toaster. The bread is the salt and pepper, but doesn't pop up.**

CENTER: **Sarsaparilla got into some real nostalgia with these classic cars. Red, (1960) Corvette and hot dog stand. 1957-Pink Thunderbird--good detail (note round window).**

BOTTOM: **Also by Vandor this pink and black record player and stack of records. Copies of the old Bakelite radios--done in ceramic.**

TOP: Sarsaparilla came out with a wonderful set with King Kong and used the same Empire State Building. Vandor had such great success with Betty Boop and her dog, Bimbo in a wooden boat, that they made another set. Betty Boop has on roller skates and is serving a hamburger, and her dog is in a bumper car.

CENTER: Betty Boop and Bimbo in wooden boat.

BOTTOM: Howdy Doody in a pink Cadillac convertible. Kit and Kat.

Clay Art, of Potrero, California, has come out with some wonderful new sets. 1989 was the 50th anniversary of the movie, "The Wizard of Oz," starring Judy Garland. These two sets of shakers depict the Wicked Witch of the West and Glinda, the Good Witch of the North, and Dorothy with Toto and the Scarecrow, and the Cowardly Lion and the Tin Man.

More fun sets from Clay Art: The princess and the frog.
Pig Gothic (not to be confused with "American Gothic"
by Grant Wood).

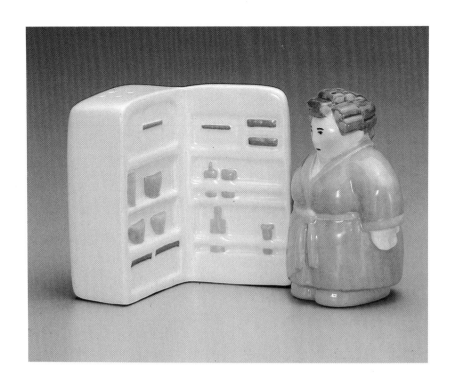

The fat lady and the refrigerator. Banana people--reminiscent of Carmen Miranda. Both by Clay Art.

TOP: The pig on the scale is by Vandor. Pilot and parachute by Sarsaparilla--this has an intricate devise for holding the parachute securely to the man.

CENTER: Two more sets by Sarsaparilla Deco Designs: Frog and horn Junior firemen-- the girl holding a dalmation, the boy a hatchet--these are very similar to the sets sold by Heather House in the 1960's--those were dressed in white.

BOTTOM: Sharpei--the wrinkled dogs from China. Dalmation and fire hydrant. Both sets from Sarsaparilla.

TOP: **A very realistic and well-crafted set of Dobermans.**

CENTER: **"Cowman Mooranda" by Vandor. Sarsaparilla calls these dogs Tailspin; they look like Spuds McKenzie.**

BOTTOM: **This dancing couple is unusual because the two shakers split at the waist instead of side by side. State of California and movie camera. Both pairs by Vandor.**

TOP: **Baseball players and Calypso singers by Clay Art.**

CENTER: **Señor Pepper--his eyes move, and his hat comes off. Pebbles and Bam-Bam from the Flintstones; there is also a set of Fred and Wilma, not shown here. By Vandor.**

BOTTOM: **Two more sets featuring black and white cows from Vandor. The cow driving the Woody station wagon is carrying his surf board on top. Christmas cow in wreath--he's sprouting reindeer horns.**

TOP: **These wrestlers by Sarsaparilla are extremely popular. A little precarious for table use, however. Bumper cars by Vandor.**

CENTER: **Marilyn Monroe by Clay Art. "Birthday Bombshell."**

BOTTOM: **Bird in hand (Sarsaparilla). Reclining cat.**

TOP: **This set would make a great "get well" gift--a chicken with a bowl of chicken soup! By Vandor.**

CENTER AND BOTTOM: **Cowboy and hat.**

JOIN THE CLUB!

Salt & Pepper
Novelty Shakers Club

Dues:
$15.00 yr. US, Canada, Mexico
$20.00 yr. UK, New Zealand, other
$5.00 extra for spousal member

Four Newsletters–Annual Convention

Information:
Irene Thornburg
581 Joy Road
Battle Creek, MI 49017
(616) 963-7954

VALUE GUIDE

Page 5
Campbell Kids $18.00-24.00

Page 6
Harvestore silos $25.00-35.00
Borden's Elsie the cow $32.00-42.00

Page 7
Mitchell's - milk bottles.........................$15.00-20.00
Wade's - milk bottles..............................$12.00-15.00
Samovar Vodka.......................................$ 6.00-10.00
Virginia Dare Beverages ....$ 6.00-10.00

Page 8
Tipo sherry ....$ 6.00-10.00
Lone Star beer ....$ 6.00-10.00
Old Milwaukee..$ 8.00-10.00
TWA...$ 8.00-10.00
Budman $35.00-55.00
Coca Cola bottles...................................$10.00-12.00

Page 9
Van Tellingen..$12.00-18.00

Page 10
Cats with sunglasses & umbrellas ....$ 8.00-10.00
Cats with bows ....$ 6.00-8.00
Tall stylized cats ....$ 8.00-10.00
Bisque Siamese cats $12.00-15.00
Holt-Howard Cats $10.00-14.00

Page 11
Lions $12.00-14.00
Leopards $12.00-14.00
Lions with fur $12.00-14.00
Scotties $25.00-35.00
Bulldog...$10.00-14.00

Page 12
Monkey $12.00-15.00
Spaniels ....$ 6.00-8.00
Cartoon animals.............................. pr.$ 6.00-8.00
Poodle ....$ 5.00-7.00
Choosie and doghouse ....pr.$15.00-18.00

Page 13
German dog & cat ....set $10.00-15.00
Dreamie and doghouse $15.00-18.00
Dachshund..$ 7.00-9.00
English Bulldogs......................................$12.00-15.00
Boston bull terriers ....pr.$ 8.00-12.00

Page 14
Dog with bone $15.00-18.00
Duck and deer..$ 8.00-10.00
Dogs with green collars...........................$10.00-12.00
Stylized zebras ....$ 8.00-10.00

Page 15
Dressed mice..$12.00-15.00
Golfing animals ....$ 8.00-10.00
Mice ....$ 8.00-12.00
Gray mouse with cheese ....$ 6.00-8.00

Page 16
Hare & tortoise ....$ 8.00-10.00
Rabbit with carrot...................................$10.00-12.00
Rabbit heads in garden...........................$12.00-15.00
New sets ....$ 6.00-8.00
Old sets $12.00-18.00

Page 17
Mother & baby cow.................................$20.00-22.00
Bear holding fish $12.00-15.00
Cartoon cows..$ 7.00-9.00
Milk cans..$ 8.00-10.00
Cows $18.00-20.00

Page 18
Buffalo $12.00-15.00
Steer...$ 8.00-10.00
Bulls $10.00-12.00
Mother and baby bear.............................$15.00-18.00
Horses ....$ 8.00-10.00
Donkeys ....$ 6.00-8.00

Page 19
Donkey & elephant $20.00-25.00
Donkeys carrying jugs ....pr.$ 8.00-10.00
Oxen $12.00-15.00
Camel, complete $25.00-30.00

Page 20
Lavender giraffe......................................$ 8.00-10.00
Nondescript donkeys ....$ 5.00-7.00
Elephant and circus tent $15.00-18.00
Elephant dressed in clothes....................$15.00-18.00
Elephants playing baseball $15.00-20.00
Cats $10.00-12.00

Page 21
Elephants..$ 6.00-8.00
Foxes..$10.00-12.00
Hippos...$10.00-12.00
Dressed Elephants..................................$10.00-12.00
Hippos...pr.$10.00-12.00

Page 22
Seals ....$ 8.00-10.00
Bears? Lambs? ....$ 6.00-8.00
Frog...$12.00-15.00
Alligators $10.00-12.00
One piece alligator $10.00-12.00
Flamingo & flower...................................$12.00-16.00

Page 23
Walrus...$12.00-15.00
Kangaroo with twins $15.00-18.00
Kangaroo with baby.................................$15.00-18.00
Sitting giraffes ....$ 8.00-10.00
Large frogs..$ 8.00-10.00

Page 24
Frog on crocodile $35.00-55.00
Frog with tomatoes $55.00-65.00
Gorillas...$ 8.00-10.00
Monkey on banana ....$ 8.00-10.00
Monkey with bowl of bananas..................$ 8.00-10.00

Page 48
Fish...pr.$ 6.00-8.00
Clams...pr.$ 8.00-10.00
Ceramic Clams ....$ 6.00-8.00
Conch shell ....$ 6.00-8.00
Red striped fish ....$ 8.00-10.00
Rainbow trout............................$ 8.00-10.00
Swordfish ....$ 6.00-8.00

Page 49
Fruit and vegetable shakers...................$ 8.00-12.00

Page 50
Cupcakes ....$ 6.00-8.00
Corn on cob................................$ 8.00-12.00
Watermelons ....$ 8.00-12.00
Watermelon & apples................$ 6.00-8.00

Page 51
Pumpkins $12.00-14.00
Squash..$12.00-14.00
Mushroom people $10.00-12.00
Cucumber people $12.00-14.00
Red peppers $12.00-14.00
Peanuts $12.00-14.00

Page 52
Lettuce people $10.00-12.00
Celery people $10.00-12.00
Googly eyes................................$ 8.00-10.00
Vegetable & fruit heads.................pr.$ 8.00-10.00

Page 53
Cheerful faces ....pr.$ 8.00-10.00
Onion heads ....$ 8.00-10.00
Tomato heads ....$ 8.00-10.00
Peas in a pod..............................$12.00-15.00
Banana & pineapple $12.00-15.00
Carrot & pea...............................$12.00-15.00

Page 54
Orange $10.00-12.00
Strawberries ....$ 8.00-10.00
Corn people ....$ 8.00-10.00
Cabbage girls..............................$ 8.00-10.00
Peas with tray $12.00-15.00
Standing Pea $15.00-18.00

Page 55
Wooden ship...............................$10.00-12.00

Page 56
Space needle................................$10.00-12.00
Peggy's cove $10.00-12.00
Mammy & Pappy jugs.................pr.$ 6.00-8.00
Flying saucers ....pr.$10.00-12.00
Rocket ship $25.00-35.00

Page 57
Minnesota ....$ 8.00-10.00
Dark green set ....$ 6.00-8.00
Connecticut ....$ 8.00-10.00
New Hampshire $10.00-12.00
USS Alabama ....$ 8.00-10.00
Missouri & mule $12.00-15.00
Suitcases.....................................$ 8.00-12.00
Pocketbooks ....$ 8.00-12.00

Page 58
Texas $10.00-12.00
1964 World's Fair $10.00-12.00
Spud potato heads......................$ 8.00-10.00
Golf balls $10.00-12.00
Teddy bears................................$ 6.00-8.00

Page 59
Cars with tray $20.00-25.00
Slot machines $10.00-12.00
Trailer & Car $12.00-15.00
Pyramid & camel $10.00-12.00
Ships...$20.00-30.00
Tanks $10.00-12.00
Cars $10.00-12.00
Airplanes $10.00-12.00

Page 60
Santas..$ 8.00-12.00

Page 61
Pumpkins $10.00-12.00
Witches $10.00-12.00
Mother's Day ....$ 8.00-10.00
Ring & license $10.00-15.00

Page 62
Bench sitters $15.00-18.00
Bride & groom $20.00-25.00
Bride & groom on altar $20.00-25.00
Wedding Bells $10.00-15.00
Ducks..$ 6.00-8.00
Girl & boy...................................$ 6.00-8.00

Page 63
Hearts ....$ 8.00-10.00
Red heart.....................................$ 8.00-10.00
Pilgrim hats ....$ 8.00-10.00

Page 64
Pilgrim man & woman $10.00-12.00
Turkeys ....$ 8.00-10.00
Santa on packages......................$10.00-15.00
Mr. & Mrs. Santa on bench......................$10.00-12.00

Page 65
Mr. & Mrs. Santa ....$ 8.00-10.00
Santa & tree $10.00-15.00
Pigs ....$ 6.00-8.00
Santa & reindeer $10.00-15.00

Page 66
Mr. & Mrs. Santa in rockers.....................$ 8.00-10.00
Santas..$12.00-15.00

Page 67
Mr. & Mrs. Santa $10.00-12.00
Church & priest..........................$10.00-12.00
Angels $10.00-12.00

Page 68
Wooden bowling.........................$ 6.00-8.00
Western ....$ 6.00-8.00
Beer bottles ....$ 5.00-7.00
Wooden chickens $12.00-15.00
Plastic canning jars ....$ 4.00-6.00
Metal Sailboats ....$ 8.00-10.00
Metal wagon & oxen..................$ 5.00-7.00

Page 90

Garden gate & hat $18.00-22.00
Mouse & trap...$20.00-22.00
Dog & food...$22.00-24.00
Violin & accordion $18.00-22.00
Purse & pocketwatch $20.00-22.00

Page 91

Sir George & dragon $24.00-26.00
Aladdin & lamp..$20.00-22.00
Bathtub & kettle......................................$20.00-22.00
Outhouse with antenna $18.00-20.00
Hat & pipe, book & glass $22.00-24.00
Diary & letters $20.00-22.00

Page 92

Ice cream & maker..................................$18.00-20.00
Cake & slice $18.00-20.00
Pipe & slippers $18.00-20.00
Brush & mug..$18.00-20.00
Roller skates...$15.00-18.00
Ice skates & sled.....................................$18.00-20.00

Page 93

Body in sand, umbrella............................$20.00-24.00
Oyster & lobster $20.00-22.00
Cowboy boots $12.00-15.00
Creel & catch $18.00-20.00
Safe & tools $24.00-26.00
Stop sign & car..$18.00-20.00

Page 94

Toys $18.00-22.00
Orange & gourd $12.00-15.00
Barbecue & Table $18.00-20.00
Telescope & saturn $18.00-20.00
Cap & diploma...$18.00-20.00

Page 95

Book & lamp..$18.00-20.00
Liberty Bell & Declaration of Independence. .$18.00-20.00
Cookbooks..$18.00-20.00
Snowman & sled......................................$18.00-20.00
Tub & soap $18.00-20.00

Page 96

Oriental pairs ....pr. $ 8.00-12.00

Page 97

Oriental boy ....$ 8.00-10.00
Oriental boy on boat $10.00-12.00
Good luck figures ....$ 8.00-10.00
Japanese women $15.00-18.00

Page 98

Men & women ....pr.$10.00-12.00
Metal figure $20.00-25.00
Hawaiian girls...$10.00-12.00

Page 99

Police...$15.00-18.00
Hawaiian couple $12.00-15.00
Dutch couples ....pr.$15.00-18.00
Children on bench $12.00-15.00
Couple in wooden shoes ....$ 8.00-10.00

Page 100

Scottish couples ....tall $10.00-12.00
....small $ 8.00-10.00
Eskimo couple...$12.00-15.00
Cartoon Eskimos ....$ 8.00-10.00
Cactus & Mexican....................................$ 8.00-10.00
Indian & tepee ....$ 8.00-10.00

Page 101

Indian & tepee $10.00-12.00
Pilgrim couple ....$ 8.00-10.00
Boy and girl $12.00-15.00
Wagon sets.....................................set $15.00-20.00

Page 102

Kitchen Witches......................................$ 8.00-10.00
Baby boxers..$10.00-15.00
Man & Woman $20.00-25.00
Boy...$18.00-22.00
Elves ....$ 8.00-10.00
Women ....$ 8.00-10.00

Page 103

Baby heads..$ 8.00-10.00
Devils...$10.00-12.00
Graduates ....$ 8.00-10.00
What's Hers $15.00-20.00
Children ....$ 8.00-10.00
Babies with flowered hats ....$ 8.00-10.00

Page 104

Young couples ....pr.$10.00-12.00
Girls $12.00-15.00
Couple..$10.00-12.00
War babies..$ 8.00-10.00
Royal couple ....$ 8.00-10.00
RCMP..$ 8.00-10.00

Page 105

Bride & groom $12.00-15.00
Young & old couple.................................$18.00-22.00

Page 106

Grandparents....................................set $12.00-15.00
Girls $15.00-18.00
Golfer $35.00-45.00

Page 107

Clown & ball...$15.00-20.00
Clown with dog.......................................$15.00-20.00
Clowns $20.00-25.00
Chefs..$20.00-25.00

Page 108

Fireman boy & girl $12.00-15.00
Bobbies $15.00-18.00
Monks...$18.00-22.00
Pirates $10.00-12.00
Sea Captains $10.00-12.00

Page 109

Sailors..$ 8.00-10.00
Friars ....$ 8.00-10.00
Nun & monk $10.00-15.00
Clowns $10.00-12.00
Lion & tamer $12.00-15.00

Schroeder's Antiques Price Guide

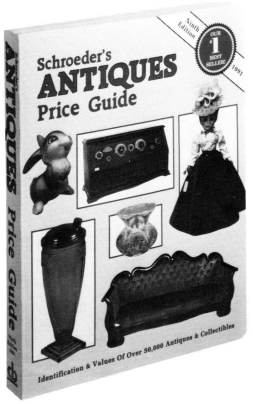

Schroeder's Antiques Price Guide has become THE household name in the antiques & collectibles field. Our team of editors work year-round with more than 200 contributors to bring you our #1 best-selling book on antiques & collectibles.

With more than 50,000 items identified & priced, *Schroeder's* is a must for the collector & dealer alike. If it merits the interest of today's collector, you'll find it in *Schroeder's*. Each subject is represented with histories and background information. In addition, hundreds of sharp original photos are used each year to illustrate not only the rare and unusual, but the everyday "fun-type" collectibles as well -- not postage stamp pictures, but large close-up shots that show important details clearly.

Our editors compile a new book each year. Never do we merely change prices. Accuracy is our primary aim. Prices are gathered over the entire year previous to publication, from ads and personal contacts. Then each category is thoroughly checked to spot inconsistencies, listings that may not be entirely reflective of actual market dealings, and lines too vague to be of merit. Only the best of the lot remains for publication. You'll find *Schroeder's Antiques Price Guide* the one to buy for factual information and quality.

No dealer, collector or investor can afford not to own this book. It is available from your favorite bookseller or antiques dealer at the low price of $12.95. If you are unable to find this price guide in your area, it's available from Collector Books, P.O. Box 3009, Paducah, KY 42002-3009 at $12.95 plus $2.00 for postage and handling.

8½ x 11", 608 Pages **$12.95**

COLLECTOR BOOKS
A Division of Schroeder Publishing Co., Inc.